MW00630424

Dad Jokes
600+ of the very best

So awful, they're actually quite funny!
Clean family-friendly humor.

Liam Oliver

Copyright © 2023
by Meca Tied Publishing
All rights reserved.

ISBN: 978-1-953561-14-5

Welcome to the ultimate collection of dad jokes! These are the very best, the crème de la crème, of dad jokes that will have you (and everyone within earshot) laughing and groaning in equal measure. This book is chock-full of clean, family-friendly humor that dads themselves have carefully honed to bring knee-slapping hilarity to loved ones and friends.

But these jokes aren't just for dads. After all, telling dad jokes and not being a dad does not make you a faux pas. So go ahead, tell dad jokes. He might even laugh!

Buckle up and get ready to embark on a journey through this funny land of dad jokes, where the puns are plentiful, the groans are guaranteed, and the laughter is contagious.

Your Review Matters

Your review could really help us get the word out about this book. This link will take you to the book's Amazon review page, where you can rate it and share your thoughts (it's okay to be brief):

rebrand.ly/reviewdadjokesbook

Thank you! As an independent publisher, we sincerely appreciate your invaluable support.

What did one elevator say to the other elevator? I think I'm coming down with something!

…

Linda broke her finger today. On the other hand, she was completely fine.

…

Did you hear about the bread factory burning down? They say the business is toast.

…

When do doctors get angry? When they run out of patients.

…

What's the difference between a poorly dressed man on a tricycle and a well-dressed man on a bicycle? Attire.

…

I was fired from a job at a calendar factory because I took a couple of days off.

…

What happens when frogs park illegally? They get toad.

…

What is the hardest part about skydiving? The ground.

…

Why did the restaurant never get off the ground? Because the chefs kept tabling everything.

…

The best gift I ever received was a broken drum. You can't beat that.

…

My wife told me to rub the herbs on the meat for better flavor. That's sage advice.

…

Why do porcupines always win the game? They have the most points.

...

I was in a grocery store when a man started to throw cheese, butter, and yogurt at me. How dairy!

...

My son is studying to be a surgeon. I just hope he makes the cut.

...

What's the difference between a pickpocket and an umpire? One steals watches and one watches steals.

...

How many months have 28 days? All of them!

...

Dogs can't operate MRI machines. But cats can.

...

I was just reminiscing about the beautiful herb garden I had when I was growing up. Good thymes.

...

My boss told me he was going to fire the person with the worst posture. I have a hunch – it might be me.

...

Why couldn't the astronaut book a hotel on the moon? Because it was full.

...

I fear for the calendar; its days are numbered.

...

I had a fun childhood. My dad used to push me down the hill in old tires. They were Goodyears.

...

What did the toilet paper roll complain about? "People just keep ripping me off!"

. . .

How do you cut the sea in half? With a seesaw!

. . .

Ever heard the rope joke? Skip it.

. . .

A magician was driving down the street and then turned into a driveway.

. . .

What's the best thing about Switzerland? I don't know, but the flag is a big plus.

. . .

Why did the raisin go out with the prune? Because he couldn't find a date.

. . .

I started a new business building yachts in my attic. The sails are going through the roof!

…

What did the digital clock say to the grandfather clock? "Look, no hands!"

…

What country's capital is growing the fastest? Ireland. Every day it's Dublin.

…

Someone stole my mood ring yesterday. I still don't know how I feel about that.

…

What runs around a baseball field but never moves? A fence.

…

What's the king of school supplies? The ruler!

…

How do you throw a party in outer space? You planet.

…

Why does Sherlock Holmes love Mexican restaurants? They give him good case ideas.

…

Why is the obtuse triangle always so frustrated? Because it's never right.

…

What would the Terminator be called in his retirement? The Exterminator.

…

My dad told me a joke about boxing, but I missed the punch line.

…

What happened when Bluebeard fell overboard in the Red Sea? He got marooned.

…

Why do bees have sticky hair? They use a honeycomb.

…

How do you fix a cracked pumpkin? A pumpkin patch.

…

What do you call a magician who loses his magic? Ian.

…

Rest in peace, boiled water. You will be mist.

…

What type of tree fits in your hand? A palm tree.

…

How are false teeth like stars? They come out at night.

…

Why can't your hand be 12 inches long? Because then it would be a foot.

. . .

What do you call an indecisive bee? A may-bee.

. . .

How was the snow globe feeling after the storm? A little shaken.

. . .

I applied to be a doorman but didn't get the job due to a lack of experience. That surprised me; I thought it was an entry-level position.

. . .

Why was the snowman looking through a bag of carrots? He was picking his nose.

. . .

What on the playground is always exhausted? The tire swing.

…

I'm practicing for a bug-eating contest, and I've got butterflies in my stomach.

…

Did you hear about the mathematician who's afraid of negative numbers? He'll stop at nothing to avoid them!

…

Can a kangaroo jump higher than the Empire State Building? Of course! Buildings can't jump.

…

Young Man: "I've come to ask for your daughter's hand in marriage." Girl's father: "You've got to take all of her or it's no deal."

…

What rock group has four men who don't sing? Mount Rushmore.

. . .

How do you deal with a fear of speed bumps? You slowly get over it.

. . .

If two vegans get in a fight, is it still considered a beef?

. . .

I, for one, like Roman numerals.

. . .

A panic-stricken man said to his doctor, "You have to help me! I think I'm shrinking!" "Now settle down," the doctor calmly told him. "You'll just have to learn to be a little patient."

. . .

Why was the coach yelling at a vending machine? He wanted his quarterback.

. . .

I used to think I was indecisive, but now I'm not sure.

…

What do you call a typo on a tombstone? A grave mistake.

…

Why should you never use "beef stew" as a password? It's not stroganoff.

…

I tried to win a sun-tanning competition. But all I got was bronze.

…

How many paranoids does it take to change a light bulb? Who wants to know?

…

What do you call corn that joins the army? A kernel.

…

What does Alexander the Great and Winnie the Pooh have in common? Same middle name.

...

Did you hear about the claustrophobic astronaut? He wanted a bit more space.

...

Do you wanna box for your leftovers? No, but I'll wrestle you for them.

...

Of all the inventions of the last 100 years, the whiteboard has to be the most remarkable.

...

What's the worst Dad joke ever? This one!

...

Don't trust that big cat. He's lion.

...

Why is grass so dangerous? Because it's full of blades.

…

How do you make the number one disappear? You add a "g" and it's "gone".

…

Why is Peter Pan always flying? He neverlands.

…

Why are fish so smart? Because they live in schools!

…

What do you call cheese that isn't yours? Nacho cheese.

…

What do you call a cow with a twitch? Beef jerky!

…

I used to work in a shoe recycling shop. It was sole-destroying.

. . .

What has to be broken before you can use it? An egg!

. . .

The new mechanic lost his job; they say he lacks fine motor skills.

. . .

What happens when a snowman throws a tantrum? He has a meltdown.

. . .

It takes guts to be an organ donor.

. . .

Where do boats go when they're sick? To the doc.

. . .

Why do seagulls fly over the sea?
If they flew over the bay, they'd be
called bagels.

…

A skeleton walks into a bar and says,
"Hey, bartender, I'll have a beer and
a mop."

…

I ate a clock the other day. It was
very time-consuming.

…

You know, people pick their nose,
but I just feel like I was born with
mine.

…

What did one monocle say to the
other? "Let's get together and make a
spectacle of ourselves."

…

Did you get a haircut? No, I got them
all cut.

…

I have a few jokes about retired people, but none of them work.

. . .

I keep trying to lose weight, but it keeps finding me.

. . .

My dad was born a conjoined twin but separated at birth. So I have an uncle, once removed.

. . .

What do you call a horse that lives next door? Neigh-bor!

. . .

They've tried to improve the efficiency of wind farms by playing country music on them, but it's not working because they're really just big heavy-metal fans.

. . .

What's the longest word in the dictionary? Smiles. There's a mile between the two S's.

...

What did the plate say to the napkin? "Dinner is on me."

...

Why didn't the skeleton go to the dance? Because he had no body to go with.

...

I won $3 million in the lottery this weekend, so I decided to donate a quarter of it to charity. Now I have $2,999,999.75.

...

What did one eye say to the other? Between you and me, something smells.

...

You used to be able to get air for free at gas stations, but now it costs $1. That's inflation for you.

…

I was going to tell a time-traveling joke, but you didn't like it.

…

What did the bald man say when he received a comb for a present? "Thanks, I'll never part with it."

…

It's not a dad bod, it's a father figure.

…

More than a century ago, two brothers decided it was possible to fly. And as you can see, they were Wright.

…

Why can't Cinderella play soccer? Because she's always running away from the ball.

…

I started a new job as a tailor last week. It's been sew-sew.

· · ·

I'm reading a horror story in Braille. Something bad is going to happen. I can just feel it.

· · ·

What do you call a crowd of chess players bragging about their wins in a hotel lobby? Chess nuts boasting in an open foyer.

· · ·

At the job interview, they asked me, "Where do you see yourself in five years?" I told them, "I think we'll still be using mirrors."

· · ·

If April showers bring May flowers, what do May flowers bring? Pilgrims.

· · ·

What's the easiest way to burn 1,000 calories? Leave the pizza in the oven.

…

How do you get a blind person to see? Usually by boat.

…

Parallel lines have so much in common. It's a shame they'll never meet.

…

Why did the toilet paper roll down the hill? Because it wanted to get to the bottom!

…

Two clairvoyants meet. One says to the other: "You are fine, but how am I?"

…

What do you get when you cross a turtle with a porcupine? A slowpoke.

…

Did you hear about the guy whose whole left side was cut off? He's all right now.

...

I was just looking at my ceiling. Not sure if it's the best ceiling in the world, but it's definitely up there.

...

What kind of award did the dentist win? A little plaque!

...

Do you know where you get water from? Well...

...

Why are basketball players messy eaters? Because they are always dribbling.

...

Did you hear about the glassblower who accidentally inhaled? He got a pane in his stomach.

...

Did you know that milk is the fastest liquid on earth? It's pasteurized before you can even see it.

…

I asked my date to meet me at the gym, but she never showed up. I guess the two of us aren't going to work out.

…

What has four wheels and flies? A garbage truck.

…

I was at the library and asked if they have any books on paranoia. The librarian replied, "Yes, they're right behind you."

…

I don't trust stairs. They're always up to something.

…

Did you hear about the two thieves who stole a calendar? They each got six months.

· · ·

Why was it called the Dark Ages? Because of all the knights.

· · ·

Ghosts are bad liars because you can see right through them.

· · ·

What do you call a line of men waiting to get haircuts? A barber-queue.

· · ·

Justice is a dish best served cold. If it were served warm, it would be justwater.

· · ·

Why are piggy banks so wise? They're filled with common cents.

· · ·

Why is the letter "A" like a flower?
Because a "B" comes after it!

...

What do you call an old snowman?
Water.

...

I just applied for a job down at the diner. I told them I really bring a lot to the table.

...

My kid wants to invent a pencil with an eraser on each end, but I just don't see the point.

...

Why is it so hard for a cucumber to become a pickle? It's a jarring process!

...

Why do melons have weddings?
Because they cantaloupe.

...

What did the judge say when the skunk walked into the courtroom? "Odor in the court!"

…

Did you hear the one about the kid who started a business tying shoelaces on the playground? It was a knot-for-profit.

…

What's orange and sounds like a parrot? A carrot.

…

How many narcissists does it take to screw in a light bulb? One. The narcissist holds the light bulb while the rest of the world revolves around him.

…

I'm reading an anti-gravity book. I can't put it down!

…

I hated facial hair, but then it grew on me.

…

Why is a dad joke like a broken pencil? Because it has no point.

…

Want to know why nurses like red crayons? Sometimes they have to draw blood.

…

A man got hit in the head with a can of soda. He's alright though – it was a soft drink.

…

Why did the tomato turn red? It saw the salad dressing.

…

I tried to start a professional hide-and-seek team, but it didn't work out. Turns out, good players are hard to find.

…

I've been watching a channel on TV that is strictly about origami. Of course, it is paper view.

. . .

I think my wife is putting glue on my antique weapons collection. She denies it, but I'm sticking to my guns!

. . .

Why was the barber disqualified after winning the race? He took a short cut.

. . .

A termite walks into a bar and asks, "Is the bar tender here?"

. . .

My teachers told me I'd never amount to anything because I procrastinate so much. I told them, "Just you wait!"

. . .

Did you hear the one about the guy with the broken hearing aid? Neither did he.

...

Why did the crab never share? Because he's shellfish.

...

Doctor: "I think your DNA is backward." Me: "AND?"

...

What gets wetter the more it dries? A towel.

...

I wanted to go on a diet, but I feel like I have way too much on my plate right now.

...

I knew a guy who collected candy canes. They were all in mint condition.

...

Last night, my wife and I watched two movies back-to-back. Luckily, I was the one facing the TV.

…

Did you know that crocodiles can grow up to 15 feet? But most only have four.

…

Why do you never see elephants hiding up in trees? Because they're really good at it.

…

Why shouldn't you write with a broken pencil? Because it's pointless.

…

"Doctor, doctor, I'm afraid of squirrels!" Doctor: "You must be nuts."

…

If it weren't for Venetian blinds, it would be curtains for everybody.

…

Why did the girl smear peanut butter on the road? To go with the traffic jam.

…

What do porcupines say when they kiss? Ouch!

…

How many apples grow on a tree? All of them.

…

My friend said to me: "What rhymes with orange." I said: "No it doesn't"

…

So what if I don't know what apocalypse means? It's not the end of the world.

…

What did the limestone say to the geologist? Don't take me for granite.

…

Why did the puppy do so well at school? Because he was the teacher's pet!

…

How many bugs do you need to rent out an apartment? Ten ants.

…

A quick shout-out to all the sidewalks out there: Thanks for keeping me off the streets.

…

Did you hear about the rancher who had 97 cows in his field? When he rounded them up, he had 100!

…

Why should you never tell a pig your secret? Because it is sure to squeal.

…

Why are mummies scared of vacation? They're afraid to unwind.

…

What do you call a multiple-choice dad joke? A pop quiz.

…

Why did the pig take a bath? Because the farmer said, "Hogwash!"

…

What is the tallest building in the world? The library – it's got the most stories.

…

Don't trust atoms. They make up everything.

…

I used to be a drill operator, but it was boring.

…

Why was the math book sad? Because it had too many problems.

…

I went to the zoo and saw a piece of toast in a cage. The sign said, "bread in captivity".

…

If a rabbit raced a cabbage, which would win? The cabbage because it's a head.

…

How do you measure a snake? In inches – they don't have feet.

…

What does a clock do when it's hungry? It goes back four seconds!

…

What did the ocean say to the beach? Nothing, it just waved.

…

Past, present, and future walked into a bar… It was tense.

…

Why did the triangle feel sorry for the circle? Because it's pointless!

…

Every time I take my dog to the park, the ducks try to bite him. That's what I get for buying a pure-bread dog.

…

How did the hipster burn his mouth? He ate his pizza before it was cool.

…

I have kleptomania, but when it gets bad, I take something for it.

…

Why are frogs always so happy? They eat whatever bugs them.

…

A kid decided to burn his house down. The boy's dad watched with tears in his eyes, turned to his wife, and said, "That's arson."

…

Why was the big cat disqualified from the race? Because it was a cheetah.

…

Can a match box? No, but a tin can!

…

Did you hear about the square that got into a car accident? Yeah, now he's a rect-angle!

…

Why haven't aliens visited our solar system yet? They looked at the reviews…only 1 star!

…

I was once fired from a canned juice company. Apparently, I couldn't concentrate.

…

What do you get from a pampered cow? Spoiled milk.

…

Does anybody know where a guy can find a person to hang out with, talk to, and enjoy spending time with? I'm just asking for a friend.

…

What's harder to catch the faster you run? Your breath.

…

Why couldn't the pirate play cards? Because he was sitting on the deck!

…

A bear walks into a restaurant and says, "I want a grilled…cheese." The waiter asks, "Why the big pause?" The bear replies, "I don't know. I was born with them."

…

Why couldn't the lifeguard save the hippie? He was too far out, man.

…

Somebody stole all my lamps. I couldn't be more de-lighted!

…

I want to go on record that I support farming. In fact, you could call me protractor.

…

How do you make a waterbed bouncier? Add spring water.

…

If at first you don't succeed, skydiving is not for you!

…

I went to a smoke shop only to discover it had been replaced by an apparel store. Clothes, but no cigar.

…

We're renovating the house, and the first floor is going great, but the second floor is another story.

…

I told my kids 10 good dad jokes to see if any of them would make them laugh. But no pun in ten did.

…

My grandfather invented the rearview mirror. Made millions – and he's never looked back since!

…

Why are skeletons so calm? Because nothing gets under their skin.

…

To whoever stole my copy of Microsoft Office, I will find you. You have my Word.

…

A friend of mine got into photographing salmon in different clothing. He said he liked shooting fish in apparel.

…

Shout-out to my fingers. I can count on all of them.

…

My new thesaurus is terrible. In fact, it's so bad, I'd say it's terrible.

…

Did you hear about the carrot detective? He got to the root of every case.

…

I knew I shouldn't steal a mixer from work, but it was a whisk I was willing to take.

…

How does the moon cut its hair? Eclipse it.

…

I used to be addicted to the Hokey-Pokey until I turned myself around.

…

Why do fathers take an extra pair of socks when they go golfing? In case they get a hole in one!

. . .

What has two legs but can't walk? A pair of pants!

. . .

Why can't a leopard hide? Because he's always spotted.

. . .

Chances are if you've seen one shopping center, you've seen a mall.

. . .

What do you get when a turkey lays an egg on top of a barn? An egg roll.

. . .

I used to have a fear of hurdles, but I got over it.

. . .

Why can't you ever run through a campsite? You can only ran – it's always past tents.

…

A backward poet writes inverse.

…

At first, I thought my chiropractor wasn't any good, but now I stand corrected.

…

My landlord told me we need to talk about the heating bill. "Sure," I said. "My door is always open."

…

How can you tell a vampire has a cold? They start coffin.

…

The butcher backed into the meat grinder and got a little behind in his work.

…

For Valentine's Day, I decided to get my wife some beads for an abacus. It's the little things that count.

...

I was offered a construction job in Egypt. Turned out to be a pyramid scheme.

...

They all laughed when I said I wanted to be a comedian. Well, they're not laughing now!

...

Have you seen a car with zero tires? It is totally unwheel.

...

A slice of mango pie is $2.50 in Jamaica and $3.00 in Puerto Rico. These are the pie rates of the Caribbean.

...

My first time in an elevator was an uplifting experience. The second time let me down.

…

Two wrongs do not make a right, but three rights make a left.

…

What is more peculiar than watching a catfish? Watching a goldfish bowl.

…

Why did the man fall down the well? Because he couldn't see that well.

…

Where do you learn to make a banana split? Sundae school.

…

What do dentists call their x-rays? Tooth pics!

…

The rotation of Earth really makes my day.

. . .

Why don't sharks eat clowns? Because they taste funny.

. . .

Why did the dinosaur cross the road? Because chickens hadn't evolved yet!

. . .

Which is faster, hot or cold? Hot, because you can catch a cold.

. . .

I just found out I'm color-blind. The news came out of the purple!

. . .

Do you want a brief explanation of what an acorn is? In a nutshell, it's an oak tree.

. . .

What did Venus say to Saturn? "Give me a ring sometime!"

…

I'm thinking about removing my spine. I feel like it's only holding me back.

…

I had a neck brace fitted years ago and I've never looked back since.

…

Two goldfish are in a tank. One says to the other, "Do you know how to drive this thing?"

…

What do you call a sad berry? A blueberry.

…

Someone glued my pack of cards together. I don't know how to deal with it.

…

Why did the stadium get so hot after the game? Because all the fans left.

…

Why did the bullet end up losing his job? He got fired.

…

I tell dad jokes, but I don't have any kids. I'm a faux pa.

…

I used to be able to play piano by ear, but now I have to use my hands.

…

Why was 2019 afraid of 2020?
Because they had a fight and 2021.

…

Why couldn't the pony sing in the choir? Because she was a little horse.

…

Why was 6 afraid of 7? Because 7, 8, 9!

…

What do you need to make a small fortune on Wall Street? A large fortune.

…

"Doctor, you've got to help me. I'm addicted to Twitter." Doctor: "I don't follow you."

…

Where did Captain Hook get his hook? From the second-hand store.

…

What did one DNA strand say to the other? "Do these genes make me look fat?"

…

What type of horses only go out at night? Nightmares.

…

I hate it when people say age is only a number. Age is clearly a word.

…

What do you call a bear with no ears? A "b".

...

What has more letters than the alphabet? The post office!

...

What was a more useful invention than the first telephone? The second telephone!

...

If a child refuses to nap, are they guilty of resisting a rest?

...

As a scarecrow, people say I'm outstanding in my field. But hay, it's in my jeans.

...

Did you hear about the king who was exactly 12 inches tall? He was a great ruler!

...

The first time I purchased a universal remote control, I thought, This changes everything!

…

What did one snowman say to another? Do you smell carrots?

…

Why don't pirates take a bath before they walk the plank? They just wash up onshore.

…

What did the grape do when he got stepped on? He let out a little wine.

…

Why do vampires have no friends? They suck.

…

What is worse than raining cats and dogs? Hailing taxis!

…

I made a belt out of watches once. It was a waist of time.

...

What did the baker say when she won an award? "It was a piece of cake."

...

I saw a thousand-year-old oil stain. It was from ancient Greece.

...

What do you call a hippie's wife? Mississippi.

...

Why is there a gate around cemeteries? Because people are dying to get in!

...

I got an email the other day teaching me how to read maps backward. Turns out it was just spam.

...

What do you give a sick lemon?
Lemon-aid.

...

To the person who stole my place in
line: I'm after you now.

...

Why is it hard to understand
volunteers? Because they make no
cents.

...

Why didn't the skeleton go to
school? His heart wasn't in it.

...

Why didn't the sun go to college?
Because it already had a million
degrees.

...

What kind of dog does Dracula
have? A blood hound.

...

When you have a bladder infection, urine trouble.

. . .

Why was the belt sent to jail? For holding up a pair of pants!

. . .

Want to hear a joke about a roof? The first one's on the house.

. . .

What do you get when the post office burns down? A case of black mail.

. . .

What makes the calendar seem so popular? Because it has a lot of dates!

. . .

I wondered why the Frisbee kept getting bigger and bigger. Then it hit me.

. . .

What's the difference between a hippo and a zippo? One is extremely big and heavy, and the other is a little lighter.

…

If you are going to try cross-country skiing, start with a small country.

…

Have you heard about those new corduroy pillows? They're making headlines.

…

I asked the IT guy, "How do you make a motherboard?" He said, "I tell her about my job."

…

My dog is a genius. I asked him, "What's two minus two?" He said nothing.

…

My wife said I should do lunges to stay in shape. That would be a big step forward.

...

What do you call cattle with a sense of humor? Laughing stock.

...

Not to brag, but I made six figures last year. I was also named worst employee at the toy factory.

...

I am terrified of elevators. I'm going to start taking steps to avoid them.

...

Wanna hear a joke about paper? Never mind. It's tearable.

...

Did you hear about the guy who invented Altoids? They say he made a mint!

...

Which side of the turkey has the most feathers? The outside.

…

The Lego shop reopens tomorrow, but I recommend avoiding it for now. People will be lined up for blocks.

…

I asked the surgeon if I could administer my own anesthetic. He said, "Go ahead, knock yourself out!"

…

On Thanksgiving Day, why did the turkey cross the table? To get to the other sides.

…

I have a joke about procrastination, but I'll tell it later.

…

I invented a new word today: plagiarism.

…

What's the least spoken language in the world? Sign language.

…

Whoever invented the knock-knock joke should get a no-bell prize.

…

I sold our vacuum cleaner. It was just gathering dust.

…

Why did the burglar hang his mug shot on the wall? To prove that he was framed!

…

What is the opposite of a croissant? A happy uncle.

…

What kind of roads do ghosts look for? Dead ends!

…

My boss told me to attach two pieces of wood together. I totally nailed it!

…

What is the leading cause of dry skin? Towels.

…

Swords will never become obsolete. They're cutting-edge technology.

…

Did you know that the first French fries weren't cooked in France? They were cooked in Greece.

…

How do you make a lemon drop? Just let it fall.

…

How many ears did Davy Crockett have? His right ear, his left ear, and his wild front ear.

…

I only know 25 letters of the alphabet. I don't know Y.

...

Why does the baker go to work? Because he kneads the dough.

...

A cheeseburger walks into a bar. The bartender says, "Sorry, we don't serve food here."

...

I had a dream that I weighed less than a thousandth of a gram. I was like, "0mg."

...

I only seem to get sick on weekdays. I must have a weekend immune system.

...

The shovel was a ground-breaking invention.

...

Why do pirates not know the alphabet? They always get stuck at "C".

…

How do celebrities stay cool? They have many fans.

…

I ordered a chicken and an egg from Amazon. I'll let you know.

…

Today, my son asked, "Can I have a bookmark?" I burst into tears – eleven years old and he still doesn't know my name is Steve.

…

What do you name an electronic encyclopedia? A facts machine.

…

What's a pirate's favorite letter? You'd think it's "R", but it's the "C".

…

I could never be a plumber. It's too hard watching your life's work go down the drain.

...

Mom: "How do I look?" Dad: "With your eyes."

...

Americans can't switch from pounds to kilograms overnight. That would cause mass confusion.

...

What did the policeman say to his belly button? "You're under a vest!"

...

If I ever find the doctor who screwed up my limb replacement surgery, I'll kill him with my bear hands!

...

Why was the robot so tired after his road trip? He had a hard drive.

...

My doctor told me I'm going deaf.
The news was hard for me to hear.

. . .

What is heavy forward but not
backward? Ton!

. . .

Fun fact: Australia's biggest export
is boomerangs. It's also their biggest
import.

. . .

How do you make an octopus laugh?
With ten-tickles!

. . .

Never play leapfrog with a unicorn
or a porcupine.

. . .

An invisible man married an
invisible woman. The kids were
nothing to look at either.

. . .

A duck walks into a pharmacy, asks for some lipstick, and says, "Put it on my bill."

...

I have a joke about a broken clock, but it's not the right time.

...

Is your refrigerator running? Then you had better go catch it!

...

Never date a tennis player. Love means nothing to them.

...

Why is it a bad idea to iron your four-leaf clover? Because you shouldn't press your luck.

...

My kid is blaming me for ruining their birthday. That's ridiculous, I didn't even know it was today!

...

Help! There's a letter coming out of the water! It's an emergin' "C"!

...

Don't tell secrets in cornfields. Too many ears around.

...

I got fired from my job as a taxi driver. Turns out customers don't appreciate it when you go the extra mile.

...

Why do bees hum? Because they don't know the words.

...

Why are toilets so good at poker? They always get a flush.

...

What do you call a dad joke when it gets old? A grandpa joke.

...

What do you call a fish with two knees? A two-knee fish!

…

Never take advice from electrons; they are always negative.

…

My writer friend claims he glued himself to his autobiography. I don't believe him, but that's his story and he's sticking to it.

…

Man, I love my furniture. Me and my recliner go way back.

…

A horse walks into a bar. The bartender says, "Hey." The horse says, "Sure."

…

Did you hear about the man who fell into an upholstery machine? He's fully recovered.

…

Why do trees look suspicious on sunny days? They just seem a little shady!

…

What kind of music do mummies love? Wrap music.

…

I startled my next-door neighbor with my new power tool. I had to calm him down by saying, "Don't worry, this is just a drill!"

…

What do a tick and the Eiffel Tower have in common? They're both Paris sites.

…

Why is the thing you're searching for always in the last place you look? Because when you find it, you stop looking.

…

My wife told me I had to stop acting like a flamingo. So I had to put my foot down!

…

The difference between a numerator and a denominator is a short line. Only a fraction of people will understand this.

…

I stayed up all night and tried to figure out where the sun was. Then it dawned on me.

…

I spent a lot of time, money, and effort childproofing my house…but the kids still get in.

…

I'm attaching a light to the ceiling, but I'm afraid I'll screw it up.

…

The other day, my wife asked me to pass her lipstick, but I accidentally passed her a glue stick. She still isn't talking to me.

…

The world tongue-twister champion just got arrested. I hear they're gonna give him a really tough sentence.

…

What do you call an alligator wearing a vest? An investigator!

…

There's not much training for garbage collectors. They just pick things up as they go.

…

Did you hear about the kidnapping at school? It's okay; he woke up.

…

I'd like to go to Holland someday. Wooden shoe?

…

The invention of the wheel was what got things rolling.

...

What do you call a shoe made from a banana? A slipper.

...

Why are fish easy to weigh? Because they have their own scales.

...

Why did the crook take a bath before he robbed the bank? He wanted to make a clean getaway!

...

What did the shy pebble wish for? That she was a little boulder.

...

A cheese factory exploded in France. Da brie is everywhere!

...

I went to the butcher's the other day and bet him $50 that he couldn't reach the meat on the top shelf. "No," he said, "the steaks are too high."

...

Why didn't the quarter roll down the hill with the nickel? Because it had more cents.

...

Why did the boy throw a stick of butter out the window? Because he wanted to see a butterfly!

...

What room does a ghost not need?
A living room.

...

Why shouldn't you tell an egg a joke?
It'll crack up.

...

No matter how much you push the envelope, it'll still be stationery.

...

How much does it cost Santa to park his sleigh? Nothing, it's on the house.

…

Why do you drive on the parkway but park on the driveway?

…

Did you hear about the restaurant on Venus? Great food, no atmosphere.

…

Two guys walked into a bar. The third guy ducked.

…

Mountain ranges aren't just funny, they are hill areas.

…

How can you tell when a bucket gets sick? It becomes a little pale.

…

A couple of yogurt cups walk into a country club and the bartender says, "We don't serve your kind here." "Why not?" one yogurt cup asks. "We're cultured."

. . .

Why can't you hear a pterodactyl go to the bathroom? Because the pee is silent.

. . .

So a vowel saves another vowel's life. The other vowel says, "Aye E! I owe you!"

. . .

What goes up but never comes down? Your age.

. . .

Did you hear the joke about the pop fly? Forget it. It's way over your head.

. . .

What did one nut say as he chased another? "I'm a cashew!"

...

Yesterday I was washing the car with my son. He said, "Dad, can't you just use a sponge?"

...

I never argue, I just explain why I'm right.

...

What is the center of gravity? The letter "v"!

...

What's green and fuzzy and will kill you if it falls from a tree? A pool table!

...

I read that by law you must turn on your headlights when it's raining in Sweden, but how am I supposed to know when it is raining in Sweden?

...

Why didn't the skeleton cross the road? Because he had no guts.

…

I finally watched that documentary on clocks. It was about time.

…

I couldn't figure out how the seat belt worked. Then it just clicked.

…

What do you call a boy named Lee who no one talks to? Lonely.

…

How do flat-earthers travel? On a plane.

…

I cut my finger shredding cheese, but I think that I may have grater problems.

…

Why is pirating so addictive? They say that once ye lose yer first hand, ye get hooked.

. . .

I just got fired from the flower shop. Apparently, I took too many leaves.

. . .

What do you call a bear who's into gardening? A Hairy Potter.

. . .

When is a door not a door? When it's ajar.

. . .

How do you get a farm girl to like you? A tractor.

. . .

What do you call two monkeys who share an Amazon account? Prime mates.

. . .

What do you call a cow that won't give milk? A Milk Dud.

…

Why did the can crusher quit his job? Because it was soda pressing.

…

Some people eat light bulbs. They say it's a nice light snack.

…

What do you call a nondescript potato? A common-tater.

…

What did the Zen Buddhist say to the hotdog vendor? "Make me one with everything."

…

Did you hear about the bankrupt poet? He ode everyone.

…

Before the invention of the wheel everything was a drag.

. . .

5/4ths of people admit they're bad at fractions.

. . .

Why are spiders so smart? They can find everything on the web.

. . .

I had a rough day, and then somebody went and ripped the front and back pages out of my dictionary. It just goes from bad to worse.

. . .

Within minutes, the detectives knew what the murder weapon was. It was a brief case.

. . .

My therapist told me I have problems expressing my emotions. Can't say I'm surprised.

. . .

What goes through every village, over mountains, crosses rivers and deserts, and yet never moves? A road.

. . .

People are usually shocked that I have a Police record. But I love their greatest hits!

. . .

What do you call a cow with no legs? Ground beef.

. . .

Stop looking for the perfect match; use a lighter.

. . .

How did the phone ask his girlfriend to marry him? He gave her a ring.

. . .

Why was the smartphone's camera blurry? It lost its contacts.

. . .

What state is known for its tiny beverages? Minnesota.

...

Straws are for suckers.

...

Why didn't the Teddy Bear eat dessert? Because he was stuffed!

...

What do sprinters eat before a race? Nothing, they fast!

...

I just bought a dictionary but all of the pages are blank. I have no words to describe how mad I am.

...

Bigfoot is sometimes confused for Sasquatch – Yeti never complains.

...

A Roman legionnaire walks into a bar, holds up two fingers, and says, "Five beers, please."

…

Sundays are always a little sad, but the day before is a sadder day.

…

What did Tennessee? The same thing as Arkansas.

…

Why was the mushroom the life of the party? It was a fungi.

…

What do you call a snobbish criminal going downstairs? A condescending con descending.

…

A weasel walks into a bar. The bartender says, "Wow, I've never served a weasel before. What can I get for you?" "Pop," goes the weasel.

…

What happened to the man who sued an airline for losing his luggage? He lost his case!

. . .

What do you call a rabbit with lice? Bugs Bunny.

. . .

I was excited to hear Apple might start making cars until I learned they wouldn't support windows.

. . .

How do you make the number seven even? Take away the "s".

. . .

I gave all my dead batteries away today, free of charge.

. . .

Someone complimented my parking today! They left a sweet note on my windshield that said, "Parking fine."

. . .

My wife asked me to go get 6 cans of Sprite from the grocery store. I realized when I got home that I had picked 7 up.

...

What washes up on very small beaches? Microwaves.

...

I burnt my Hawaiian pizza today. I should have set the oven to aloha temperature.

...

What did the older light bulb say to the younger light bulb? "You're too young to go out tonight."

...

An angry bird landed on a doorknob. Then it flew off the handle.

...

What did the 0 say to the 8? "Nice belt."

…

I never wanted to believe that my dad was stealing from his job as a road worker. But when I got home, all the signs were there.

…

Why does Norway have barcodes on their battleships? So when they get back to port, they can Scandinavian.

…

Yesterday, a clown held a door open for me. I thought it was a nice jester.

…

What did one wall say to the other wall? "I'll meet you at the corner."

…

Spring is here! I got so excited that I wet my plants.

…

What do you call an ant that has been shunned by his community? A socially-dissed ant.

...

I can tolerate algebra, maybe even a little calculus, but geometry is where I draw the line.

...

I had a dream that I was a muffler last night. I woke up exhausted!

...

If Whole Foods sells sliced apples, is it false advertising?

...

Why did the pencil cross the road? It was lead!

...

I have a joke about chemistry, but I don't think it will get a reaction.

...

What do you get when you divide the circumference of a jack-o-lantern by its diameter? Pumpkin Pi!

...

Did you hear about the eyeglasses maker who moved his shop to an island off Alaska and is now known as an optical Aleutian?

...

I was going to get a brain transplant, but I changed my mind.

...

What did the buffalo say to his little boy when he dropped him off at school? Bison.

...

Granddad always told me things could be worse. He'd say I could fall into a deep hole full of water, but I knew he meant well.

...

How do you get straight A's? By using a ruler!

…

Why couldn't the bicycle stand up by itself? It was two-tired.

…

I have a friend who drives a steamroller. He's such a flatterer.

…

How come a man driving a train got struck by lightning? He was a good conductor.

…

Why did the actor fall through the floorboards? He was going through a stage!

…

It's hard to explain puns to kleptomaniacs because they take everything literally.

…

My boss told me to have a good day,
so I went home.

…

My seasickness comes in waves.

…

A man dug three holes and said,
"Well, well, well…"

…

I told my doctor I heard buzzing,
but he said it was just a bug going
around.

…

To the guy who invented zero:
Thanks for nothing.

…

What does a house wear? Address.

…

What do you get when you cross
an elephant with a fish? Swimming
trunks.

…

Why do pancakes always win in baseball? They have the best batter.

…

What did Marie say about her brain surgeon? "I really gave him a piece of my mind!"

…

What did the finger say to the thumb? "I'm in glove with you."

…

Why is "dark" spelled with a "k" and not a "c"? Because you can't "c" in the dark!

…

Broken guitar for sale. No strings attached.

…

What word starts with "E" and has only one letter in it? Envelope.

…

What is the difference between ignorance and apathy? I don't know and I don't care.

…

What should you do if someone rolls their eyes at you? Roll them back!

…

The shoe said to the hat, "You go on ahead, and I'll follow on foot."

…

What did Adam say on the 24th of December? It's Christmas, Eve.

…

Why is it a bad idea to insult an octopus? Because it is well-armed.

…

I lost 25% of my roof last night…oof.

…

What's the difference between a pun and a dad joke? Dad jokes are punnier.

…

Why did the quiz show give away $10,000 plus one banana? They wanted the prize to have appeal.

…

What type of haircut do bees get? Buzzcuts!

…

Every day I tell my wife I'm going to jog around the neighborhood, but I never do. It's a running joke we have.

…

Why was the student's report card wet? It was below "C" level!

…

What do you call a man named David without an ID? Dav.

…

If you think swimming with dolphins is expensive, you should try swimming with sharks. It cost me an arm and a leg!

...

Thanks for explaining the word "many" to me; it means a lot.

...

I saw an ad in a shop window: "Television for sale, $1, volume stuck on full." I thought, I can't turn that down.

...

My new sweater had a problem with static, so I returned it. They gave me a new one free of charge.

...

Why couldn't the couple get married at the library? It was all booked up.

...

Why do elephants never use computers? Because they're afraid of mice.

...

Do you know where you can get chicken broth in bulk? The stock market.

...

Shout-out to my grandma; that's the only way she can hear.

...

The best time on a clock is 6:30 – hands down.

...

What happens when a strawberry gets run over crossing the street? Traffic jam.

...

My wife is really mad at the fact that I have no sense of direction. So I packed up my stuff and right.

...

Why did the kid throw his clock out the window? Because he wanted to see time fly!

…

Teacher: "John, where are the Great Plains?" John: "At the airport."

…

How does a penguin build a house? Igloos it together.

…

When I started telling dad jokes like my father, I knew I was full-groan.

…

Did you hear about the campsite that was visited by Bigfoot? It got in tents.

…

What's the best time to go to the dentist? Tooth-hurty.

…

Why does Humpty Dumpty love autumn? Because Humpty Dumpty had a great fall.

…

Are monsters good at math? Not unless you count Dracula.

…

I have a joke about a roof, but it would just go over your head.

…

My wife and I had an argument about which vowel is the most important. I won.

…

Lance isn't that common a name these days, but in medieval times, they were called lance-a-lot.

…

I quit my job at the coffee shop the other day. It was just the same old grind over and over.

…

A boiled egg is hard to beat.

…

Why was the baby ant confused? Because all his uncles were ants.

…

Guy told me today he did not know what cloning is. I told him, "That makes two of us!"

…

What did the tie say to the hat? "You go on ahead. I'll hang around."

…

Dad, can you explain to me what a solar eclipse is? No sun.

…

Friend: "Bro, can you pass me that pamphlet?" Me: "Brochure."

…

What do you call a sleeping bull? A bulldozer.

…

What do you call HIJKLMNO? H2O

...

What creature is smarter than a talking parrot? A spelling bee.

...

I was a bookkeeper for 10 years. The local librarians weren't too happy about it.

...

Cooking out this weekend? Don't forget the pickle. It's kind of a big dill.

...

Imagine if you walked into a bar and there was a long line of people waiting to take a swing at you. That's the punch line.

...

How did Darth Vader know what Luke Skywalker got him for his birthday? He felt his presents.

...

Why did the boy tiptoe past the medicine cabinet? He didn't want to wake up the sleeping pills!

...

A good steak pun is a rare medium well done.

...

What's the difference between Bad Jokes and Dad Jokes? One starts with "B" and the other starts with "D".

...

Why do standup comedians perform poorly in Hawaii? Because the audience only responds in a low ha.

...

Do mascara and lipstick ever argue? Sure, but then they makeup.

...

I'll tell you what often gets overlooked: garden fences.

...

Why did the house go to the doctor? It was having window panes.

…

How do you get a good price on a sled? You have toboggan.

…

Did you hear the rumor about butter? Well, I'm not going to spread it!

…

My mouth has turned into a flower bed. It has tulips.

…

Why is the Mississippi River unusual? Because it has four eyes and can't see!

…

You know what they say about cliffhangers…

…

If a pig loses its voice, does it become disgruntled?

…

I thought about going on an all-almond diet. But that's just nuts.

…

Plateaus are the highest form of flattery.

…

Why aren't dogs good dancers? They have two left feet.

…

Why did the invisible man turn down the job offer? He couldn't see himself doing it.

…

How are opera singers and sailors alike? They both have to handle the high C's!

…

Our wedding was so beautiful, even the cake was in tiers.

…

What is a monster's favorite dessert? I scream.

…

How much does it cost a pirate to get his ears pierced? About a buck an ear.

…

Want to hear a joke about going to the bathroom? Urine for a treat.

…

I wouldn't buy anything with Velcro. It's a total rip-off.

…

My favorite word is "drool." It just rolls off the tongue.

…

If the Pilgrims were alive today, what would they be most famous for?
Their age.

. . .

Why did Mozart sell his chickens?
They kept saying, "Bach, Bach, Bach."

. . .

A book just fell on my head. I only have my shelf to blame.

. . .

What is an astronaut's favorite key on a computer keyboard? The space bar.

. . .

Where should you go in the room if you're feeling cold? The corner – they're usually 90 degrees.

. . .

Show me a piano falling down a mine shaft, and I'll show you A-flat minor.

...

Archaeology really is a career in ruins.

...

What do you call a factory that makes products that are just average? A satisfactory.

...

Not sure if you've noticed, but I love bad puns. That's just how eye roll.

...

Where do animals go when their tails fall off? To the retail store!

...

Why are elevator jokes so good? Because they work on so many levels.

...

I was fired from the keyboard factory yesterday. I wasn't putting in enough shifts.

· · ·

I wish I could clean mirrors for a living. It's just something I can see myself doing.

· · ·

Which days are the strongest? Saturday and Sunday. The rest are weekdays.

· · ·

What music frightens balloons? Pop music!

· · ·

Are snails faster without their shells? No, they're more sluggish!

· · ·

Why do we tell actors to "break a leg"? Because every play has a cast.

· · ·

I'm on a seafood diet. I see food and I eat it.

...

Why is no one friends with Dracula? He's a pain in the neck.

...

A guy walks into a bar. And that's how he lost the limbo contest.

...

How do you know if a joke is a dad joke? A dad joke has to reach father for a pun.

...

Your Review Matters

Your review could really help us get the word out about this book. This link will take you to the book's Amazon review page, where you can rate it and share your thoughts (it's okay to be brief):

rebrand.ly/reviewdadjokesbook

Thank you! As an independent publisher, we sincerely appreciate your invaluable support.

Made in the USA
Columbia, SC
15 June 2023

18148364R00061